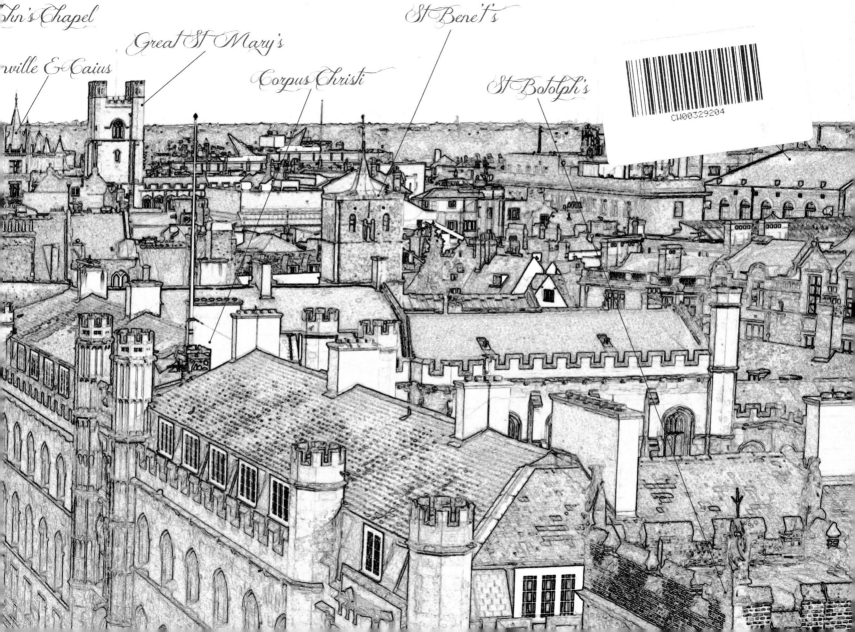

ohn's Chapel

Great St Mary's

St Bene't's

nville & Caius

Corpus Christi

St Botolph's

Cambridge

A city for all seasons

Photography by Andrew Pearce

Fotogenix Publishing

First published in Great Britain 2017
@Fotogenix Publishing
01767 677086
www.fotogenix.co.uk

All photography @ Andrew Pearce; Fotogenix
Design & editing by Debi Pearce
Fonts: Cormorant, WWDesigns, Jellyka Delicious Cake

Printed by Swallowtail in Norfolk

ISBN 978-0-9547355-5-5

Contents

Left: The "Mathematical" Bridge, Queens' College
Right: Cloisters in New Court, St John's

Advice from a Candid Friend, 1673

"Do not go to Cambridge, Sir,
there are Alehouses, in which you will be drunk.
There are Tennis-Courts, and Bowling Greens that
will heat you to an excess, and then you will
drink cold small Beer and die.
There is a River, too, in which you will be drowned,
and you will study yourself into a Consumption,
or break your Brain."

Left: Historic towers of Cambridge
Following page: St John's Backs

1209 ∷ Scholars arrived, escaping riots in Oxford

1284 ∷ Peterhouse founded by Bishop Hugh de Balsham

1338 ∷ University Hall (1326) refounded as Clare College

1347 ∷ Pembroke College

1348 ∷ Gonville Hall

1350 ∷ Trinity Hall

1352 ∷ Corpus Christi founded by townspeople

1428 ∷ Benedictine monks' hostel created, known as Buckingham College

1441 ∷ King's College endowed by Henry VI

1446 ∷ Foundation stone of King's Chapel laid by Henry VI

1448 ∷ St Bernard's College (1446) refounded as Queens' College

1473 ∷ St Catharine's College

1496 ∷ Jesus College

1505 ∷ God's House (1439) refounded as Christ's College

1511 ∷ St John's College

1542 ∷ Buckingham College refounded as Magdalene College

1546 ∷ Trinity College founded by Henry VIII

1584 ∷ Emmanuel College: the first Puritan foundation

1596 ∷ Sidney Sussex: the second Puritan College

1730 ∷ Senate House completed

1762 ∷ Foundation of first Botanic G...

6

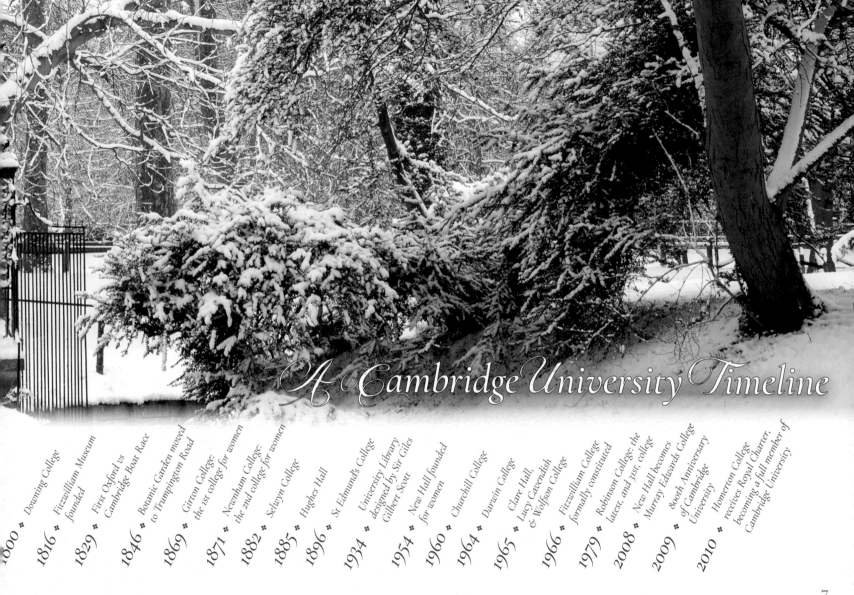

A Cambridge University Timeline

1800 ∷ Downing College

1816 ∷ Fitzwilliam Museum founded

1829 ∷ First Oxford vs Cambridge Boat Race

1846 ∷ Botanic Garden moved to Trumpington Road

1869 ∷ Girton College: the 1st college for women

1871 ∷ Newnham College: the 2nd college for women

1882 ∷ Selwyn College

1885 ∷ Hughes Hall

1896 ∷ St Edmund's College

1934 ∷ University Library designed by Sir Giles Gilbert Scott

1954 ∷ New Hall founded for women

1960 ∷ Churchill College

1964 ∷ Darwin College

1965 ∷ Clare Hall, Lucy Cavendish & Wolfson College

1966 ∷ Fitzwilliam College formally constituted

1979 ∷ Robinson College: the latest, and 31st, college

2008 ∷ New Hall becomes Murray Edwards College

2009 ∷ 800th Anniversary of Cambridge University

2010 ∷ Homerton College receives Royal Charter, becoming a full member of Cambridge University

Some Cambridge Nobel Prize Winners

Year	Name, College	Field	Achievement
1904	Lord Rayleigh, Trinity	~ Physics ~	Discovered Argon
1906	J. Thomson, Trinity	~ Physics ~	Electrical conductivity of gases
1925	Austen Chamberlain, Trinity	~ Peace ~	Work on the Locarno Pact
1927	Charles Wilson, Sidney Sussex	~ Physics ~	Invented the cloud chamber
1933	Paul Dirac, St. John's	~ Physics ~	Work on quantum mechanics
1935	James Chadwick, Caius	~ Physics ~	Discovered the neutron
1945	Ernst Chain, Fitzwilliam	~ Medicine ~	Discovered Penicillin
1947	Edward Appleton, St John's	~ Physics ~	Discovered the Appleton Layer
1950	Bertrand Russell, Trinity	~ Literature ~	'A History of Western Philosophy'
1958	Frederick Sanger, St John's	~ Chemistry ~	Structure of the Insulin molecule
1959	Philip Noel-Baker, King's	~ Peace ~	Work towards global disarmament
1962	Francis Crick, Caius/Churchill James Watson, Clare Maurice Wilkins, St John's	~ Medicine ~	Determined the structure of DNA
1964	Dorothy Hodgkin, Newnham/Girton	~ Chemistry ~	Structure of compounds used to fight anaemia
1972	John Hicks, Caius	~ Economics ~	Equilibrium theory
1979	Allan Cormack, St John's	~ Medicine ~	Developed CAT scans
1984	Richard Stone, Caius	~ Economics ~	Developed national accounting system
2002	Sydney Brenner, King's	~ Medicine ~	Discoveries concerning genetic regulation of organ development and cell death
2009	Venkatraman Ramakrishnan, Trinity	~ Chemistry ~	The structure and function of the ribosome

Early crocus along the Backs, near King's Chapel

Peterhouse

founded in 1284 by Bishop Hugh de Balsham:
the first Cambridge College

Two sides of the same story!
Poet Thomas Gray describes his move from Peterhouse to Pembroke College
in a letter to a friend, 25th March 1756:

"I left my lodgings because the rooms were noisy, and the People of the house dirty ... All I shall say more is, that I am for the present extremely well lodged here, and as quiet as in the Grand Chartreuse; and that everybody ... are as civil as they could be to Mary de Valence in person."

Rev. John Sharp, of Peterhouse, was less than sympathetic
in his own account on March 12, 1756:

"This case is much talked of, and is this. He is much afraid of fire ... he has ever since kept a ladder of rope by him, soft as the silky cords by which Romeo ascended to his Juliet, and has had an iron machine fixed to his bedroom window. The other morning, Lord Percival and some Petrucheans, going a hunting ... thought it would be no bad diversion to make Gray bolt, as they called it, so ordered their man Joe Draper to roar out fire. A delicate white nightcap is said to have appeared at the window: but finding the mistake, retired again to the couch. The young fellows, had he descended, were determined, they said, to have whipped the butterfly up again."

Above: Peterhouse's new Whittle Building
Opposite: Daffodils in Peterhouse Deerpark

Fitzwilliam College

originally Fitzwilliam House, founded 1869;
received full University status in 1966

*10th November 2011 ~ Ken Olisa speaks to
Varsity's Emilia Korczynska about his funding of
Fitzwilliam's new Olisa Library, opened in 2010:*

"My time at Fitzwilliam was transformative for a state school boy from the poor streets of Nottingham. The College's welcoming and egalitarian atmosphere and Cambridge's academic excellence gave me the privileged experiences which underpin my career. It seems only right to repay some of that privilege by helping Fitz and its students to achieve their potential."

Right: The Olisa Library
Opposite: Distinctive architecture by Sir Denys Lasdun

Sidney Sussex College

founded in 1596 by Lady Frances Sidney, Countess of Sussex

*Oliver Cromwell entered Sidney Sussex as a student on April 23rd 1616,
but later treated the College members cruelly during the Civil War.
The College bitterly recorded beside his name in the student admissions book:*

"This was that great impostor, that most accursed butcher, who when the most pious King Charles had been disposed of by foul murder, usurped the throne itself, and for the space of almost five years, under the name of Protector, tormented the three kingdoms with unrestrained tyranny."

Above: The College cloisters reflect its monastic origins
Opposite: A rural haven, hidden in the centre of town

Lucy Cavendish College

founded in 1965

From Newspresenters Ltd, 2015 - a new College President is appointed:

"Lucy Cavendish College, University of Cambridge, is delighted to announce the election of Jackie Ashley as the new President, from Autumn 2015. Jackie Ashley, 60, has been a high-profile political journalist and commentator for ITN, Channel 4 News, the BBC, the New Statesman and the Guardian. She also sits on a number of boards, including University College London Hospitals' Biomedical Research Council; Birkbeck College, University of London's Centre for the Study of Politics; and Women in Sport.

She said yesterday: 'All my working life, I have been campaigning for better rights for women. I've been involved in campaigns for equal pay, carers, older women, and on health issues' ... Lucy Cavendish College was founded 50 years ago by some remarkable women research academics, one of whom was a computer pioneer. Its mission has been to broaden access to top-quality university education, and to provide women over 21 with the opportunity to achieve their academic ambitions and fulfill their potential.

'At a time when access to elite institutions has become such a hot political topic; and when women are still earning substantially less than men for similar jobs, I cannot think of a more exciting place to be working. There is nowhere quite like Lucy Cavendish College. I am proud to be becoming its leader and champion'."

Clare Hall

founded in 1965

Cambridge News, 7th March 2016, Adam Care reports:

"When physicist Dr David L Gosling was offered a job as principal of a university college in Pakistan's lush Peshwar province it was an offer he could hardly refuse ... However all that changed when a drone strike hit a nearby madrassa, killing 85 local boys ... The attack heralded four years of chaos, as a resurgent Taliban sought retribution across the troubled Afghan border region. Keen to ensure life continued as normal, Dr Gosling continued his mission to promote education, particularly of women, to the anger of the local Taliban...

He said: 'Supporting women's participation in Pakistan is quite controversial, and after about a year I got a death threat ... I could see it was unjust that women in that region are discriminated against. When people at the college disagreed I didn't try and argue for the rights of women as they would have regarded that as a western thing. I said look at the results. Twelve per cent of the students were women, but they were carrying away 53 per cent of our top prizes, and they couldn't argue with that'.

After surviving Taliban attacks and increasing drone strikes, he returned to Cambridge and to Clare Hall. His book covers the four years he spent in Pakistan ... He said: 'I thought it might be helpful to counteract some of the misconceptions people have. That was my main motivation, to speak up for the people and give them a voice'."

Queens' College

founded in 1448 by Margaret of Anjou, wife of King Henry VI

In 1511, Dutch Theologian Desiderius Erasmus was invited to stay and teach at Queens'
by the Master, Bishop John Fisher. His letters to a friend during August and October that year
reveal a longing for the comforts of home:

"I shall stay some days at least in this college. I have not yet submitted myself to
an audience, for I am anxious to take care of my health first. I do not like the ale
of this place at all, nor are the wines particularly palatable. If you could manage
to send me a cask of Greek wine, the very best that can be bought, you would be
doing your friend a great kindness, but mind that it be not too sweet."

...

"I am sending back your cask, which I have kept with me longer than I otherwise
should have done, that I might enjoy the perfume at least of Greek wine. My
expenses here are monstrous, and not a farthing to be gained. I have spent here not
quite five months, and yet spent sixty nobles; while certain members of my class
have presented me with just a single one ..."

Above: Erasmus' octagonal tower
Opposite: The 'Mathematical' Bridge

19

Selwyn College

founded in 1882

Cambridge News, 6th January 2016 - Adam Care reports:

"2016 marks the 40th anniversary of women students and fellows first being admitted to Selwyn College, which is now planning to introduce some new additions to its hall. More than 30 photographic portraits of current students and staff have been commissioned to mark the anniversary, with a dozen of them set to be hung in the dining hall and an adjoining room from today, alongside paintings of former male fellows and dons.

College master Roger Mosey told the News the decision had been unanimously approved by its ruling council. He said: 'We have been planning a celebration for 40 years of women at Selwyn for a few months now, and one of the ideas was to have portraits of current women. Other colleges have done similar things, but it just struck us it would be nice to have pictures of contemporary women'."

Right: The Greek inscription 'Quit ye like men'
Opposite: Cherry avenue in Selwyn's exceptional gardens

Emmanuel College

founded in 1584 by Sir Walter Mildmay

Henry Gunning, Senior Squire Bedell in the mid 1800s, describes Emmanuel's bicentennial celebrations. From his 'Reminiscences of Cambridge':

"On the 29th September, 1784, Emmanuel College celebrated the 200th anniversary of its foundation. The entertainment was of the most superb description. Several lively turtles were to be seen in tubs of water, at the Master's Lodge, where the people were allowed for some days to gratify their curiosity with a sight so novel in Cambridge. Upon one occasion a woman who had been looking at them very attentively, said - 'Pray, Sir, are them real turtles or mock turtles?'"

Left: Paddock's pond dates from the 13th century Dominican friary
Opposite: The Chapel was designed by Sir Christopher Wren in 1677

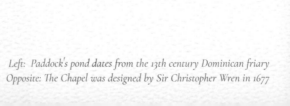

Murray Edwards College

founded in 1954 by Cambridge University

The Independent, 28th August 2008,
Hilary Wice reports:

"A bitter fight has broken out in Cambridge over the decision by one of the women's colleges to change its name. New Hall announced at the end of last term that it was to become Murray Edwards College after receiving a £30m endowment from a former graduate, Ros Smith, and her husband Steve Edwards, both software entrepreneurs...

The college says that New Hall was only ever a temporary name while it sought financial backing, and that the new name has been chosen to honour the benefactors and the college's founder, Dame Rosemary Murray. But protesting alumnae point out that the new benefactors never asked for a name change, and are also furious that the college, which was founded to champion women's education, should be taking on a man's name."

Left: The College's distinctive neo-Byzantine dome
Opposite: The 'Transit of Venus' garden design, entered in the 2007 Chelsea Flower Show

The Botanic Garden

created in 1846 by John Henslow, teacher of Charles Darwin

Philomena Guillebaud recalls her school days:

"Between 1932 and 1938 I attended a small school in Panton Street run by a Mrs Smith. She had obtained permission from the Director of the Botanic Garden for her pupils to run about on the big lawn during their morning break, and each day if it was not raining, we walked, accompanied by Miss Henn the junior mistress, in a school crocodile up Panton Street and into the Garden, where we followed the path round past the hothouses to the lawn.

Outside one of the hothouses was a cactus bristling with spines on broad leaves like pingpong bats, and one day a little boy called Johnny Lindgren fell into the cactus and had to be whisked off to the doctor to get the spines removed. Ever after, Miss Henn stationed herself beside the plant, reciting "Mind the cactus! Mind the cactus!" rather like a hen preparing to lay an egg."

Tom Hulley expresses gratitude for the healing power of plants:

"I have made friends and been befriended by so many trees in the gardens that it is not fair to pick a favourite. On a recent visit, I had a touch of migraine caused by the dazzling sun. Looking for a shady bench, I realised that many of the seats in the gardens are set in the sun.

Eventually I found a still, dark and slightly chilly place and sat down with closed eyes. After a while, there was a gentle stroking on my head, a kind caress, and I realised that Zelkova was comforting me. On many occasions I have had a quiet word with this fine tree and its friend the Hop Hornbeam and its huge close neighbour the Wingnut. They make a particularly impressive trio. Anyway, it seems that trees have memories as well as good will. Thanks Zelkova, my migraine was gone within minutes of your touch."

The
King's Boat Club

On a damp windy day
In tempestuous May,
In a most insufficient attire,
What a pleasure to row
For a furlong or so,
And to glow with a patriot's fire:
There is glory to win in the fray,
There are crowds to applaud all the way,
We shall very soon be
At the top of the tree
If we all go out every day.

Let's all go out every day
From now till the middle of May!
We shall very soon be
At the top of the tree
If we all go out every day.

By the top of the tree,
As I think you must see,
It's the head of the river I mean:
An appropriate place
For our vessel to grace
At which she will shortly be seen:
There are still a few boats in the way,
But Rome was not built in a day,
And I have no doubt
We shall bring it about
If we all go out every day.

Right: St Catharine's, pursued by Pembroke

Says our captain, says he:-
'May you all of you be
Dissected and roasted and skinned:
Five rowed with his back
In the shape of a sack
And then, when I swore at him, grinned:
Six, get those hands sharper away!
Keep your eyes in the boat there, I say!
Now get on to it, do!
Get that body down, Two!
Your time's worse than ever to-day.'

Both our Tutors are there,
Neither pleasure nor care
Can keep them away from the scene:
And who shouteth so loud
In that jubilant crowd,
As each blown† but uproarious Dean?
The Provost brings down Mrs A,
Who runs a good part of the way;
Our Proctor himself
Throws his bands on the shelf
And dismisses his staff for the day.

Let's all go out every day
From now till the middle of May!
We shall very soon be
At the top of the tree
If we all go out every day.

⁓⟷⟷

James Kenneth Stephen, 1880

†*blown: out of breath*

Girton College

founded in 1869 by
Emily Davies, Barbara Bodichon & Lady Stanley

The Independent, 30th May 1998 -
Suzannah Chambers reports:

"When Elizabeth Layton graduated from Cambridge University 62 years ago, she was so thrilled that she did not mind that her name was not on the degree ceremony list. After three years studying economics at Girton College, she felt honoured to be sent a certificate in the post - even though it was only a titular degree.

Women in the class of 1936 were not the first to be denied the honour of graduating with a full Cambridge degree that would make them members of the university.

From the first intake of female students in 1869, until 50 years ago, women had to make do, at best, with mailed university certificates. Now Cambridge is at last to recognise those women's achievements with a ceremony in July, to be attended by more than 900 of them."

Jesus College

founded in 1496 by Bishop John Alcock

John Strype, (1643 - 1737), a freshman at Jesus College in 1662, writes home to his mother:

"GOOD MOTHER, - the reason y⁰ receive this no sooner is, because I had a mind ... that this honest woman should deliver it into yʳ hands, yᵗ so y⁰ may better and more fully heare of me, and know how it fareth with me. She is my laundresse make her welcome, and tell her how y⁰ would have my linen washed. Mother I kindly thank y⁰ for yʳ orange pills y⁰ sent me. If you are not to straight of mony send me some such thing by the Woman, and a pound or two of Almonds and Raisons. But first ask her if she will carry yᵐ, or if they will not be to much trouble to her ...

I understand by yʳ Letter yᵗ y⁰ are very inquisitive to know how things stand wᵗʰ me here. My breakings out are now all gone, indeed I was affraid at my first coming it would have proved yᵉ Itch: but I am fairly rid of it: But I fear I shall get it, let me do what I can: for there are many here yᵗ have it cruelly. Some of yᵐ take strong purges yᵗ would kill a horse, weeks together for it, to get it away, & yet are hardly rid of it. At my first coming I laid alone : but since, my Tutour desired me to let a very clear lad lay with me and an Alderman's son of Colchester, wᶜʰ I could not deny, being newly come : he hath laid with me now for almost a fortnight, and will do till he can provide himself with a Chamber.

Wee go twice a day to Chappell; in the morning about 7, and in the evening about 5. After we come from Chappell in yᵉ morning wᶜʰ is towards 8, we go to yᵉ Butteries for our breakfast, wᶜʰ usually is 5 farthings; an halfpeny loafe and butter, & a cize of beer. But sometimes I go to an honest House neere yᵉ Coll., and have a pint of milk boyled for my breakfast. "

Above: The College is approached via a narrow walled path called 'The Chimney'
Opposite: Jesus' renowned wisteria in First Court

32

Wolfson College

By Matthew Reisz, 12th November 2013
matthew.reisz@tsleducation.com

"Founded as University College in 1965 to accommodate research students, it acquired its present name in 1973 after a major donation from the Wolfson Foundation. In the same year, a wealthy Singaporean pineapple grower, Lee Seng Tee, brought his daughter to study there. When he was given a lift to the railway station by the college's tutor, plant pathologist Peter Lowings, Dr Lee started describing the terrible problems he was having on his plantation.

Dr Lowings sent some research students to take a look, and they discovered the plantation had been infected by bacteria transmitted by ants. In gratitude for this invaluable help, Dr Lee donated funds to build an assembly hall, a new library and a garden. The pineapple connection is commemorated in a mural painted for the college's 40th anniversary."

Right: Wolfson's new buildings were opened in 1977 by Queen Elizabeth II
Opposite: The Lee Library, opened in 1994

Corpus Christi College

founded in 1352 by the town guilds of Corpus Christi and the Blessed Virgin Mary

Edmund Spenser, 1552 - 1599, himself of nearby Pembroke College, describes a grass-cutting machine:

"There on the grasse within this goodlie court,
A hideous monster fed with horrid tongue,
Ne knight with such a dragon-whelp had fought,
Ne poet such prodigious birth had sung;
And up and down it pass'd the grasse among;
And still with fearful sownd its teeth did grind
That all the bodies nerves and fibres wrung;
Its bellie low upon the earth did wind,
Four human legs before, and eke a pair behind.

And much in sooth this sownd the clerkes opprest,
And did confound them in their studie quight,
Albeit no fear their bodies e'er possest,
The creature would not scratch, ne tear, ne bite,
(Certes its sownd would almost kill outright)
And manie a charm they try'd within their ken,
To ease them from its power by day and night;
For well 'twas thought it was three proper men
Bound by some evil bond which might be broke agen,

Which quickly Geomet perceived trew,
And hasten'd to dissolve the cruell spell,
For gentle pity mov'd him, when he knew
The creature did no harm, but worken well;
Nathless the awefull noyse no tongue may tell;
Then loud he shouted out the magick word,
'Beere! Beere!' the yron from the bodie fell,
The curse was broke, the monster's corps was stirr'd,
Uprose three goodlie men: the sownd no more was heard."

Above: Pelican detail from the chapel altar cloth
Opposite: Corpus Chapel: its architect, William Wilkins, chose this, his favourite building, for his burial-place

Robinson College

founded in 1979 by entrepreneur and philanthropist, Sir David Robinson

Cambridge News, 11th December 2016 - Chris Elliot reports:

The Rosie Maternity came into being in 1983, thanks to a £3 million donation by David Robinson, the Cambridge-born businessman who became one of the city's greatest ever benefactors… When the construction start date was pushed right to the back end of the Eighties, David Robinson did not think Cambridge's expectant ladies should have to wait that long, so he stepped in and made his gift, on the condition that work began without delay, and that the new hospital was opened quickly too.

David, later Sir David, was the son of Cambridge bike shop owner Herbert Robinson. Born in 1904, he first worked for his father before moving to Bedford to found his own garage business, and then branched out into the radio and television rental business. He set up a chain of successful shops … that made him a millionaire, and later he became a hugely successful horse-racing owner as well. And then he gave all his money away. He set up a charitable trust, and in an astonishing outpouring of philanthropy, built a swimming pool for the people of Bedford, opened an arts centre at his old school, funded a new wing at the Evelyn Nursing Home in Cambridge, handed over a pile of money to pay for heart surgery at Papworth, and bankrolled the creation of a new Cambridge college, the one named after him. Oh, and he bought four lifeboats as well.

The Rosie – named after Sir David's mother, who tragically died in childbirth – opened in 1983.

Left: Robinson is built from 1.25 million handmade bricks,
Opposite: Bin Brook forms a charming natural feature

Fireworks at the May Balls

Ruey, of The Ruey Review, compares the extravaganzas at Trinity and St John's in the rueyreview.blogspot.co.uk, 17 July 2012:

"Fireworks is one of the biggest draws for the May Balls at Trinity and St John's. The fireworks at both colleges were amazing. They were both choreographed with music. It still boggles my mind to this day how University-affiliated colleges like the mentioned two go to such lengths to arrange firework shows that are more extravagant and elegant than the ones put on on national days in most countries around the world. So, the two colleges are quite competitive over the issue of who has the better fireworks each year. Apparently St John's college, usually having its May Ball the day after Trinity's, holds money in reserve each year to 'up' Trinity upon observing the Trinity fireworks the previous night. Therefore, the conventional understanding is that John's has better fireworks than Trinity. Personally, this year I thought it was a tie. I think it is true that John's fireworks is more epic, but that does not make Trinity fireworks any less impressive in terms of extravagance and elegance. In the Trinity May Ball you do get a much better view of the fireworks as you can watch on one side of the river while the fireworks shoot up into the sky on the other, at very close range. Whereas in John's you just get to watch a very impressive show on a large field without the River Cam being a part of the experience. At Trinity you can see the plebs who are not in the actual ball sitting in their punts on the River Cam looking up into the sky wishing that they can one day watch the fireworks on land. Moreover, Trinity had flamethrowers which were big pluses. I personally enjoyed the Trinity May Ball fireworks better because of the venue, but I do recognize that John's fireworks was much bigger and Michael Bayer. So I say the fireworks showdown was a tie."

Senate House

designed by architect James Gibbs, completed in 1730

*Philosopher William Paley, 1743 ~ 1805, warns agains the pitfalls
of the University's competitive academic environment.*

"You may do anything with young men by encouragement, by prizes, honours and distinctions; see what is done at Cambridge. But there the stimulus is too strong; two or three heads are cracked by it every year ... some of them go mad, others are reduced to such a state of debility, both of the mind and body, that they are unfit for anything during the rest of their lives."

*Opposite: Exam results are displayed on noticeboards
outside Senate House*

Homerton College

became an official Cambridge College in 2010
*Poet Laureate and Honorary Fellow, Carol Ann
Duffy, writes for Homerton's 2010 celebrations:*

Homerton

Home is in Homerton
and you can find the moon
concealed in Homerton,
a hidden light revealed.
Respice finem.

Merit in Homerton,
if you will have an eye
only for Homerton,
a lovely sight revealed.
Respice finem.

Respice finem.
Look to the end.
The last act crowns the play.
Respice finem
and Homerton the way.

Hero in Homerton.
Mother, alma mater,
and more in Homerton,
a bright new morn revealed.
Respice finem.

Respice finem.
Look to the end.
The last act crowns the play.
Respice finem
and Homerton the way,
Homerton the way.

Hughes Hall

began in 1885 at Croft Cottage in Newnham; received a Royal Charter, making it officially a Cambridge College, in 2006

"A woman's place is wherever she wants."

"We shall never get first-rate education until men and women are trained together."

These are the words of Elizabeth Phillips Hughes, first Principal of Hughes Hall. She was a determined and foresighted advocate of co-education, rather than solely women's equal status. She worked to develop a strong international network for sharing of ideas on education. Between 1885 and 1899 she succeeded in training over 500 women teachers at Hughes Hall. In 1948 the University admitted women as full members for the first time. To mark this occasion, the college changed its name to honour Miss Hughes. In the 1970s it was the first all-women college to admit men, and today has an almost equal balance of male and female post-graduate students from 68 different countries. Miss Hughes would certainly approve!

Grantchester

*Before her ill-fated marriage to poet Ted Hughes,
Sylvia Plath captures fleeting happiness in a letter
to her mother during her time at Cambridge in
the 1950s:*

"Got up at 4.30 am this day with Ted and
went for a long walk to Grantchester ... I
felt a peace and joy in the most beautiful
world with animals and birds ... We
began mooing at a pasture of cows, and
they all looked up, and as if hypnotised,
began to follow us in a crowd of about
twenty across the pasture to a wooden
stile, staring fascinated. I stood on the
stile and, in a resonant voice, recited all I
knew of Chaucer's Canterbury Tales for
about twenty minutes. I never had such
an intelligent, fascinated audience."

Left: The mill pool - Grantchester's mill burnt down in 1928
Opposite: High Summer in Grantchester meadows

Clare College

refounded in 1338 by Lady Elizabeth de Clare

from The Express, 6th April 2016:

"Broadcasting legend Sir David Attenborough got himself into a bit of a flap as he abseiled down a 50-foot high wall at his old university. The fearless naturalist, who turns 90 next month ... returned safely to terra firma having taken to the air to get a birds' eye view of a 'living wall' at Cambridge University's David Attenborough Building. His gravity-defying stunt was to mark the creation of a new global hub for the largest cluster of nature conservation groups and university researchers in the world.

Sir David - who studied natural sciences at Cambridge in the 1940s - has links with many of the organisations based there and agreed to the abseil to promote their work. He said: 'The future of our life on Earth is dependent on the natural world - for the air we breathe, the food we eat and the water we use - and for the feelings we have of awe and wonder at nature's extraordinary riches. In this remarkable age we are learning more and more about the intricacies of our dependence on nature.

'Yet our natural world is threatened as never before. By bringing together leaders in research, practice, policy and teaching, we stand the greatest chance of developing the solutions required to save our planet. I am enormously proud that these collaborations are occurring in a building bearing my name'."

Right: Clare Fellows' gardens, designed in 1947 by E.N. Willner; Trinity Hall is glimpsed beyond, to the left.

Magdalene College

founded in 1428

Samuel Pepys records the installation
of his library at the college, August 24th 1666:

"Up, and despatched several businesses at my home in
the morning, and then comes Simpson to set up my other
new presses for my books: and so he and I fell to the
furnishing of my new closett†, and taking out the things
out of my old; and I kept him with me all the afternoone,
till it was quite dark, hanging things, - that is, my maps,
and pictures, and draughts, - and setting up my books,
and as much as we could do, to my most extraordinary
satisfaction; so that I think it will be as noble a closett
as any man hath, and light enough, - though, indeed, it
would be better to have had a little more light."

†library

Right: The College motto, meaning 'keep your faith'
is humorously interpreted as 'mind your liver!'
Opposite: Samuel Pepys' library

Christ's College

founded in 1505 by Lady Margaret Beaufort

*Mr. Mead of Christ's College writes during a 'visitation' of the plague,
in a letter dated 24th April 1630:*

"Our University is in a manner wholy dissolved: all meetings & Exersises ceasing. In many Colledges almost none left. In ours of 27 Mess[†] we have not five. Our Gates strictly kept, none but Fellowes to go forth, or any to be lett to without y[e] consent of the major part of our Society, of w[ch] we have but 7 at home at this instant, only a Sizer may go with his Tutors Ticket upon an errand. Our Butcher, Baker and Chandler bring y[e] provisions to the Colledge Gates, where the Steward and Cooke receive them. We have taken all our Officers into the Colledge & none must stirre out. If he doth he is to come in no more. Yea we have taken 3 Women into our Colledge & appointed them a Chamber to lye in together. Two are Bedmakers, one a Laundresse. I hope the next Parlement will include in y[e] generall Pardon. We have turned out our Porter & appointed our Barber both Porter and Barber, allowing him a Chamber next y[e] Gates. Thus we live as close Prisoners, & I hope without danger."

† *In late Middle English this term denoted any of the small groups into which the company at a banquet was divided (who were served from the same dishes); hence, 'a group who regularly eat together'.*

Above: Christ's gate displays the ornate Beaufort coat of arms
Opposite: Hydrangeas gracing Christ's Fellows' Building, 1642

Some notable Cambridge names

Charles Babbage, Henry Cavendish, Richard Baker	Peterhouse
Hugh Latimer, David Attenborough, John Rutter	Clare
Nicholas Ridley, William Pitt, Bill Oddie	Pembroke
William Harvey, John Venn, Alastair Campbell	Gonville & Caius
Admiral Howard, J.B. Priestley, Stephen Hawking	Trinity Hall
Christopher Marlowe, Matthew Parker	Corpus Christi
Samuel Pepys, Charles Kingsley, A. C. Benson	Magdalene
Francis Walsingham, John Maynard Keynes, Salman Rushdie	King's
Desiderius Erasmus, Isaac Milner, Stephen Fry	Queens'
John Addenbrooke, Ian McKellen, Jeremy Paxman	St Catharine's
Thomas Cranmer, Alastair Cooke, Prince Edward	Jesus
Charles Darwin, Jan Smuts, Sacha Baron-Cohen (Ali G.)	Christ's
Abdus Salam, William Wilberforce, Douglas Adams	St John's
Isaac Newton, Rajiv Ghandi, Prince Charles	Trinity
John Harvard, Cecil Parkinson, Graeme Garden	Emmanuel
Oliver Cromwell, David Owen, Carol Vorderman	Sidney Sussex
John Cleese, Brian Redhead, Quentin Blake	Downing
Sylvia Plath, Germaine Greer, Emma Thompson	Newnham
John Selwyn Gummer, Hugh Laurie, Clive Anderson	Selwyn

Opposite: Punts resting by Garret Hostel Bridge

Gonville & Caius

founded in 1348 by Edmund Gonville, & refounded by John Caius in 1557

In the mid 1500s, Puritan zeal was at its height, and many people felt it necessary to demonstrate their aversion to Catholicism by violently destroying the 'superstitious' images and objects associated with its rituals. Dr John Caius was a staunch Catholic. The University's vice-chancellor, Dr Byng, describes his raid on Caius' rooms to the chancellor, Lord Burghley, in a letter dated December 14th, 1572:

"I am further to give your honor advertisement of a greate oversight of D. Caius, who hath so long kept superstitious monumentes in his college, that the evill fame thereof caused my lord of London to write very earnestly unto me, to see them abolished. I could hardly have been persuaded that suche thinges by him had been reservid. But, causing his owne company to make searche in that college, I received an inventory of muche popishe trumpery ... as might have furnished divers massers at one instant. It was thought good, by the whole consent of the heades of howses, to burne the books, and such other thinges as served most for idolatraous abuses, and to cause the rest to be defacid; whiche was accomplished yesterday, with the willing hartes as appeared of the whole company of that howse."

Dr Caius resigned six months later, devastated. He died on 29th July 1573, aged 63. His own account of the raid (originally in Latin), dated 13th December 1572 recounts:

"Outrageously he treated them, cutting them in pieces, casting them on the fire, and assailing them with horrible names and epithets ... what they could not burn they broke and defaced with hammers ... So great was their religious fervour, that neither personal entreaty, nor the dignity of the Academy could persuade them to treat the building and the books with moderation."

Above: The College layout forms a series of small courts, linked by Dr Caius' three symbolic Gates representing Humility, Virtue and Honour
Opposite: The statue of benefactor Dr Stephen Perse holds an effigy of the school that he also founded

Newnham College

founded in 1875 by the Association for Promoting
the Higher Education of Women in Cambridge

*In 1897 University members voted on whether to grant degrees to women
(662 in favour, 1,713 against). Male undergraduates staged ribald demonstrations,
involving mockery of a female effigy on a bicycle. The figure was later decapitated.
The Cambridge Daily News, 21st May 1897, reports:*

"A vigorous cock crowing from the roof of Caius College, emanating from an enterprising undergrad, and done with marvellous fidelity, was the sign for the commencement of operations. Forthwith the occupants of the front rooms of Caius began to hang out their banners on the outer walls, and a roar of laughter went up as there slowly descended from an upper window the lay figure of a woman with aggressively red hair, dressed in cap and gown. As the figure swung to and fro in the breeze, limp and lank, the remarks made were the reverse of complimentary to the sex ... At the corner of the Market-place the effigy of a woman arrayed in blue bloomers and pink bodice, sitting astride a bicycle, was run out from an upper window and received with cheers and groans."

*Opposite: Architect Basil Champneys designed Newnham's buildings
in the elegant 'Queen Anne' style*

59

Trinity Hall

founded in 1350 by Bishop William Bateman

The chimes for Big Ben in London were originally composed for Great St Mary's in Cambridge. An article on English bell chimes in The Spectator, 2nd April 1870 relates:

"Before we take our leave of the work under notice, it will not be amiss to note that its author has raked up the composer of those extremely beautiful chimes which all Cambridge men remember at Great St Mary's, and which have been borrowed at the Royal Exchange, and in scores of other places ... It seems that in 1793, (at Trinity Hall) when Crotch was one of the pupils of Dr Randall, then Regius Professor of Music, the Regius Professor of Law, Dr Jowett, was something of a practical mechanician. Of this Jowett it was said:-

> *A little garden little Jowett made,*
> *And fenced it with a little palisade;*
> *If you would know the taste of little Jowett,*
> *This little garden won't a little show it.*

Jowett appears to be entitled to the credit of the clockwork, and Crotch to that of the music. It was said, by a fellow pupil of Crotch's, that when the chimes were first heard, they were thought so strange that they were nicknamed *Jowett's Hornpipe.*"

Left: Trinity Hall's distinctive crescent motif is also featured on milestones along the route to London, funded by the College in 1730
Opposite: The College is noted for its bijou riverside gardens

Trinity College

founded in 1536 by King Henry VIII

Reverend Adam Sedgwick (1785-1873) describes Queen Victoria's visit in 1843:

"By one o'clock the members of the University were marshalled in our Great Court, to the number of more than 2000, in silent and solemn order. At length, at about two o'clock ... the Royal Standard was seen to rise slowly and majestically over the great gateway. For a moment all was silent as death; each man was drawing in his breath that he might with more energy send forth a shout of gratulation. I never heard such a shout before, reverberated as it was from every corner of our noble court ... where the Master and Seniors were met to do homage, and present to their sovereign the College keys. You never saw such an ample bunch of keys - large, ponderous, and rusty - and strapped together by an old greasy bit of leather - thick enough to have bound the limbs of unshaven Samson, and looking as if it had been cut from the flank of a rhinoceros. Her Majesty contemplated this phenomenon with eyes of wonder, and then gently waving her Royal hand signified thereby her will that the ponderous bunch should be restored to the keeping of the Bursar. On the carriage moved towards our Lodge door - order was at an end - the whole University moved like a great wave, and threatened some dire confusion; but the front rank halted at a respectful distance, so firmly that no act of disorder was committed. The very tumult, and the sudden condensation of the Academic mass, only added to the heartiness and joyousness of the greeting."

Above: Trinity's library, designed free of charge by Sir Christopher Wren
Opposite: Great Court was created in 1593 by Thomas Nevile, who had the entire clock tower moved back 20 feet to align with the chapel

Trinity College

'The same, but not the same' -
In his poem, 'In Memoriam', 1850, Alfred, Lord Tennyson revisits his
old college following the death of his dear friend Arthur Hallam:

... "I past beside the reverend walls
In which of old I wore the gown;
I roved at random through the town,
And saw the tumult of the halls;

And heard once more in college fanes
The storm their high-built organs make,
And thunder-music, rolling, shake
The prophet blazon'd on the panes;

And caught once more the distant shout,
The measured pulse of racing oars
Among the willow; paced the shores
And many a bridge, and all about

The same gray flats again, and felt
the same, but not the same; and last
Up that long walk of limes I past
To see the rooms in which he dwelt.

Another name was on the door:
I linger'd; all within was noise
Of songs, and clapping hands, and boys
That crash'd the glass and beat the floor ..."

Right: Trinity's Avenue was first planted in 1672
and renewed in 1949
Opposite: Trinity's founder, King Henry VIII

St Edmund's College

founded in 1896 by Henry Fitzalan Howard -
the first Catholic college in Cambridge for 224 years

From Varsity, 30th May 2016, by Haroun Mahmud

"Over 300 Cambridge academics have signed a letter arguing against Britain leaving the European Union, weeks before the referendum on the 23rd June...

With the debate about Britain's continuing membership of the European Union becoming increasingly fraught in national media, the letter draws attention to the benefits the academic community and young people draw from the UK being part of the continent-wide union of 28 member states. The letter argues that British universities, ranked among the most successful centres of learning and research anywhere in the world, are "significantly helped by support and funding from the EU"... It also highlighted that young Britons gain a considerable amount from having access to EU scholarships, stressing "the importance of the free exchange of ideas, research and information that is made possible by the free movement of academics within Europe".

The letter was organised by Matthew Bullock, who since 2014 has been the Master of St Edmund's College. The 307 signatories represent a cross-section of different faculties, ranging from the humanities and language departments to the sciences."

66

Left: Beyond the trees St Edmund's tower, built in 1993, has a commanding view of the city

Churchill College

founded in 1959 by Sir Winston Churchill - the first co-educational college in Cambridge. Its intent was to create a college for a new age, uniting science and industry

Sir Winston Churchill, 1874-1965

"I trust and believe that this College, this seed that we have sown, will grow to shelter and nurture generations who may add notably to the strength and happiness of our people, and to the knowledge and peaceful progress of the world. The mighty oak from an acorn towers; a tiny seed can fill a field with flowers'."

Right: Churchill's Møller Centre for management training

St John's College

founded in 1511 by Lady Margaret Beaufort

Whipplesnaith, the voice of Cambridge University's daring, secret 'Nightclimbers',
advises on the ascent of St John's New Court tower, 1937:

"Following the leads round, one has to step from one battlement to the next at the corner. Rather unexpectedly after the quiet walk round one finds one's self looking down for fifty feet straight below. Then along by New Court, up some slates, on to a ledge and over some more battlements and one is at the foot of the tower.

We chose the face down which comes the lightning conductor ... From a man's shoulders one can stand with a foot on each buttress, because they slope away from the vertical. One can now reach a ledge to the front and above one's head. A scramble lands one on a sort of terrace, a yard wide and two yards long. If the climber be alone, he can manage this first part by taking one of the neighbouring faces, where a clockless circle of stone provides the necessary holds ...

The next twelve feet are the most difficult part of the climb. There are windows on each face of the Tower. The Tower becomes a couple of yards narrower in diameter at the foot of these windows. Pillars rear up at the outside corners and are joined to the Tower by an arch of sloping stone, festooned on the upper side with ornamentations that should not be trusted too far. The difficulty is to get up the length of the pillar. At arm's length above, wedge-shaped tongues of stone pointing downwards give some help, but not a complete hold. The window was divided down the middle by a verical bar of stone ... Place a foot as high as possible on this bar. Then, making as much use as possible of the semi-hold above, place a foot on the pillar behind and straddle the gap. From now on it is merely a wriggle to get on to the arch, and the rest is practically a stone ladder to the pinnacle."

Above: New Court's 'Wedding Cake' tower
Opposite: New Court's magnificent Virginia creeper

Queens' College

founded in 1448 by Queen Margaret of Anjou, wife of King Henry VI

Even before he became Lord Protector in 1653, Oliver Cromwell carried out a tireless crusade against Catholicism. While Member of Parliament for Huntingdon in the 1640s, his fanatical assistant, William Dowsing, carried out work on his behalf in the county, destroying symbols of Catholicism wherever he could. Dowsing's 'Journal' is a catalogue of the destruction he brought about. His entry dated December 26, 1643, reads:

"We beat downe about 110 Superstitious Pictures besides Cherubims and Ingravings, where none of the Fellows would put on their Hatts in all the time they were in the Chapell & we digged up the Steps for 3 hours and brake down 10 or 12 Apostles and Saints within the Hall."

Left: Queens' medieval gate tower
Opposite: The 'Mathematical' bridge

Downing College

founded in 1800 by Sir George Downing

*The shadow of War: from the Michaelmas issue of
Downing College's magazine, 'The Griffin', 1914:*

"Looking back to the end of last term, we remember that
every prospect seemed good this year; there was no hint of
the trouble to come ... we looked forward with confidence to
great happenings, whilst a fair crop of academic distinction
seemed probable. But it was not to be. In August the call
came, and the call was answered ... One by one the rest
came up; in little groups we foregathered, discussing the
all-compelling topic, and watching to see who would be with
us, and who would not. But those who came up were few;
on every hand, we miss the wonted number of our friends.
Daily we are reminded of them in untenanted room and silent
stair, and the empty seats in Hall speak eloquently of their
numbers. So many have gone, so many of those whom the
College could ill spare; and still others go. Our thoughts are
of them, and, whether on the field of battle, or bearing their
part still near at home, our good wishes go with them."

*Right: Downing's unique classical architecture
Opposite: Downing's vast grounds occasionally serve as
a landing place for University visitors arriving by helicopter*

The American Cemetery at Madingley

Dedicated on 16th July, 1956

Remembered by Louis T. Stanley in his book 'Life in Cambridge':

"This time I observed the Two Minutes Silence on the wooded hill of Madingley within sight of the towers and spires of Cambridge. Tall, slim trees guarded the entrance-drive. On the other side the fields sank gently from the ridge towards the village. A morning mist still lingered ghost-like in the trees. Beyond was a sight that brought home with sharpness the bitter-sweetness of remembered things. I looked across the fields and saw row upon row of white marble crosses - an army of almost 4,000 American Servicemen on their last parade.

The simplicity of those gleaming Italian marble crosses was an unspoken prayer. Here and there the outline was broken by the Star of David. Almost every State was represented. Men from Texas, Tennessee, Virginia, Arizona, Oregon, Montana, Minnesota, California and Georgia lay at rest in the soil of Cambridge.

The American flag moved in the wind as if fingers were plucking the folds. In the distance came the sound of a gun. A group of workmen by the Chapel bared their heads. The Silence was broken only by the cawing of rooks - a silence frozen in memory spanning 3,000 miles of ocean."

Above: 3,812 headstones mark the final resting-place of American servicemen
Opposite: The Cemetery was set out on land donated by Cambridge University

Darwin College

jointly founded in 1964 by St John's, Trinity, and Gonville & Caius

Bill Gates, on Darwin Alumnus Sir David MacKay
From gatesnotes, the blog of Bill Gates, 3rd May 2016:

"I was sad to learn last month that David MacKay had died of cancer. He was just 48 years old. David was well known among those who study clean energy, and he had a big influence on a lot of people, including me... I discovered David through his eye-opening book Sustainable Energy-Without the Hot Air. He was a physicist at Cambridge University, and his goal was to, as he put it, cut 'UK emissions of twaddle' by helping people think more rigorously and numerically about clean energy ...
A few years ago, when I gave a TED talk on energy, I bought 2,000 copies to pass out to everyone in the audience ... I had the pleasure of getting to know David and learning from him...(Although he was a knight, he never went by Sir David.) I will miss him a lot, but I am grateful that he left behind so much fantastic work. It is a fitting legacy."

Left, & Opposite: Darwin's oldest building, Newnham Grange, was bought in 1885 by Sir George Darwin along with the Old Granary

King's College

founded in 1446 by King Henry VI

Charles Darwin (1809-1882) recalls the uplifting music in King's Chapel

"I also got into a musical set ... From associating with these men, and hearing them play, I acquired a strong taste for music, and used very often to time my walks so as to hear on week days the anthem in King's College Chapel. This gave me intense pleasure, so that my backbone would sometimes shiver. I am sure there was no affectation or mere imitation in this taste, for I used generally to go by myself to King's College, and I sometimes hired the chorister boys to sing in my rooms. Nevertheless I am so utterly destitute of an ear, that I cannot perceive a discord, or keep time and hum a tune correctly; it is a mystery how I could possibly have derived pleasure from music ... But no pursuit at Cambridge was followed with nearly so much eagerness or gave me so much pleasure as collecting beetles."

Above: King's fountain is topped by a statue of its founder Henry VI

Opposite: Cattle often graze in the pasture by King's Chapel

King's College

founded in 1446 by King Henry VI

King's Fellow Rupert Brooke recalls his alma mater -
from a letter to his friend A.F Schofield in 1913:

"My heart is sick for several things
Only to be found in Kings ...

I do recall those haunts with tears,
The Backs, the Chapel, and the Rears ...
O places of perpetual mire,
Localities of my desire,

O lovely, o remembered gloom
And froust of Chetwynd lecture room ...
O spots my memory is gilding,
O Jumbo Arch! O Wilkins Building! ...

Haunts where I drank the whole damn night!
Place where I catted till the light!
Dear spot where I was taken short,
O Bodley's Court, O Bodley's Court!"

Above: Spires of King's Great Gate, designed
by William Wilkins

Opposite: Autumn mist by Bodley's Court

81

A King's Timeline

1441	—	Henry VI founds college
1446	—	Foundation stone of chapel laid
1461	—	Henry VI captured & chapel abandoned
1485	—	Richard III defeated by Henry VII - 5 bays of the chapel completed
1506	—	Henry VII recommences work
1512	—	Chapel shell finished & roofed
1515	—	Main structure & vaulting completed
1536	—	Chapel first used for service
1644	—	Chapel used as a drill hall by Cromwell's soldiers
1724	—	Fellows' Building designed by James Gibbs
1818	—	Existing stone bridge installed
1822	—	William Wilkins adds screen
1873	—	Non-Etonians admitted for 1st time
1879	—	Fountain & statue of Henry VI added to Front Court
1893	—	Bodley's Court completed
1928	—	1st broadcast of Festival of 9 Lessons & Carols
1965	—	'Peace in Vietnam' banner suspended from chapel
1972	—	King's becomes co-educational
2014	—	Fellow Alan Turing's pioneering work in computers & mathematics acknowledged by a blue plaque at the college

Right: Winter sunset, King's College Chapel

King's College

King Henry VI conceived his grand designs for King's College when he was only 18.
He was an immensely popular monarch whose untimely end
brought him the status of unofficial sainthood. His modest, devout nature
is clearly illustrated in his own prayer:

"O Lord Jesu Christ, who didst create me,
redeem me and fore-ordain me unto that which now I am;
thou knowest what thou wilt do with me;
deal with me according to thy most compassionate will.
Amen."

Left: King's Chapel is famed for its Christmas broadcast of the
Festival of 9 Lessons and Carols, first transmitted in 1928

St John's College

founded in 1511 by Lady Margaret Beaufort, grandmother of Henry VIII

Thomas Lever, (1521-1577) praises the dedicated scholars of St John's
in his sermon preached at St Paul's Cross, December 14, 1550:

"There be dyuers ther whych ryse dayly betwixte foure and fyue of the clocke, vse common prayer wyth an exhortacion of gods worde in a commune chappel, and from sixe vnto ten of the clocke vse euer eyther pryuate study or commune lectures. At ten of the clocke they go to dynner, whereas they be contente wyth a penye pyce of byefe amongst foure, having a fewe porage made of the brothe of the same byefe, wyth salte and otemell, and nothing els.

After thys slender dinner they be either teachynge or learnyng vntyll five of the clocke in the euenyng, when as they haue a supper not much better than theyr dyner. Immedyatelye after the whyche, they go eyther to reasoniyng in problemes or vnto some other studye, vntyll it be nyne or tenne of the clocke, and there beyng without fyre are fayne to walk or runne vp and down halfe an houre, to gette a heate on their feete whan they go to bed.

These be menne not werye of theyr paynes, but very sorye to leue theyr studye: and sure they be not able some of them to contynue for lack of necessarye exibicion and relese. These be the lyuing sayntes whyche serue god takyng great paynes in abstinence, studye, laboure, and dylygence, wyth watching and prayer."

Above: The Bridge of Sighs, 1831
Opposite: St John's Chapel & Third Court

St John's College

William Wordsworth describes his favourite tree at the college in his
autobiographical poem, 'The Prelude', written circa 1800:

..."All winter long, whenever free to choose,
Did I by night frequent the College grove
And tributary walks ... Lofty elms,
Inviting shades of opportune recess,
Bestowed composure on a neighbourhood
Unpeaceful in itself. A single tree
With sinuous trunk, boughs exquisitely wreathed,
Grew there: an ash, which Winter for himself
Decked out with pride, and with outlandish grace:
Up from the ground, and almost to the top,
The trunk and every master branch were green
With clustering ivy, and the lightsome twigs
and outer spray profusely tipped with seeds
That hung in yellow tassels, while the air
Stirred them, not voiceless. Often have I stood
Foot-bound uplooking at this lovely tree
Beneath a frosty moon ..."

Above: Trees remain a significant feature of
St John's extensive grounds
Opposite: St John's New Court via Trinity Bridge

St Catharine's College

founded in 1473 by Robert Wodelark

Thomas Hobson (1544-1631) was a well-known Cambridge figure who ran a stables and carrying service from premises which now form part of St Catharine's. His portrait, kept at the college, depicts him plainly dressed, but with a large money bag!
Poet John Milton seems to have been fond of Hobson, as he wrote several epitaphs for him, including one which accompanies the portrait:

"Laugh not to see so plaine a Man in print.
The shadow's homely, yet ther's something in't,
Witnes the Bagg he wear's though seeming poore
The fertile Mother of a thousand more :
He was a thriveing Man, through lawful Gaine,
And wealthy grew by warrantable paine ;
Then laugh at them that spend, not them y^t gather,
Like thriveing Sonnes of such a thrifty Father."

Above: The College emblem is the spiked wheel of St Catharine, intended for her execution, which broke in answer to her prayers
Opposite: The College is affectionately known as "St Cat's"

Pembroke College

founded in 1347 by Marie de St Pol, Countess of Pembroke

Bishop Nicholas Ridley, (1500-1555) played an active role in Henry VIII's Reformation. He paid dearly for it when Henry's vengeful Catholic daughter, Mary Tudor, had him burned at the stake in Oxford. While in prison just prior to his execution on 16th October 1555 he wrote:

"Farewell Pembroke Hall, of late mine own colledge my care and my charge; what case thou art in now, God knoweth, I know not well. Thou wast ever named since I knew thee (which is now thirty years ago) to be studious, well-learned, and a good setter forth of Christ's gospel, and of God's true word, so I found thee, and blessed be God so I left thee indeed. Wo is me for thee mine own dear colledge, if ever thou suffer thyself by any means to be brought from that trade. In thy orchard (the walls, buts and trees, if they could speak would bear me witness) I learned without book almost all Paul's Epistles, yes, and I ween all the Canonical Epistles, save only the Apocalyps of which study although in time a great part did depart from me, yet the sweet smell thereof I trust I shall carry with me into heaven, for the profit thereof I think I have felt in all my life time ever after, and I ween of late, (whether they abide there now or no I cannot tell), there was that did the like. The Lord grant that this zeal and love towards that part of God's word, which is a key and a true commentary to all the holy scripture, may ever abide in that colledge so long as the world shall endure."

Left & Opposite: The College grounds have evolved as a series of distinctive gardens from different eras

Clare College

founded as University Hall in 1326 by Richard de Badew
& refounded in 1338 by Lady Elizabeth de Clare

Lady Elizabeth, 3 times widowed, died on 4th November 1360.
Her wisdom and foresight regarding her college is clearly shown in the
Preamble to the Statutes of the Foundress, 1359:

"Elizabeth de Burgh, Lady of Clare, to all children of Holy Mother Church who read these words:

greeting and remembrance of our deed! Experience, the universal guide, plainly shows that learning is no mean advantage in every rank of life, ecclesiastical or civil. Though many people seek it in many ways, it is best acquired in a recognised university community; and when its pupils have acquired it and tasted its sweets, it sends them out well qualified to rise according to their merits to different ranks in church and state. But so many men have been swept away by the ravages of the plague that learning has lately suffered a sad decline in numbers. We, therefore, desiring to assist true religion and to further the public good by promoting learning so far as God has put it in our power to do so, have turned our attention to the University of Cambridge in the diocese of Ely, where there is a body of students. Our purpose is that through their study and teaching at the university they should discover and acquire the precious pearl of learning, so that it does not stay hidden under a bushel but is displayed abroad to enlighten those who walk in the dark paths of ignorance. And to enable the scholars residing in our said college to live in harmony under the protection of a firm discipline and so enjoy greater freedom to study, we have with the advice of experts made certain statutes and ordinances, set out below to stand in perpetuity."

Above: The College's elegant buildings were constructed
between 1638 & 1715
Opposite: Clare's bridge is the oldest in Cambridge, completed in 1638

Epilogue

At school I detested History. When Fotogenix Publishing began over twenty years ago I would have laughed at the idea that, in 2017, I would be working on my 8th Cambridge book project. And yet, somehow along the way, I have developed an emotional bond with the historic figures I encounter during my research. Too often I am obliged to pare my text down to the barest facts, with no room for the human detail which has brought the town's old stonework alive for me. Here perhaps, I may give a voice to those monochrome names printed in the textbooks, whose own words give a deeper sense of life in Cambridge than mine ever could.

I have acknowledged the sources of my quotations throughout the book, but must pay tribute here to a few in particular. I owe a debt of gratitude to John Willis Clark of Trinity College, whose thorough work at the end of the 19th century forms the rock on which I build my own. In this book, another Trinity man, Sydney Waterlow, has provided many ancient transcripts in his own anthology of 1912, *In Praise of Cambridge*. I am especially grateful to Adam Care, correspondent for the *Cambridge News*, for many modern sources.

I have uncovered so many personal tales of tragedy and celebration, desperate acts, and quiet courage, missing the comforts of home, and the thrill of new adventures. Human emotion is a constant that spans the centuries to unite us all. Despite our modern technology, we still face threats of war and pestilence, not to mention the insidious encroachment of climate change. It would take very little to erode our delicate veneer of civilisation and return us to the fear and violence of former times glimpsed in these pages. The tales derived from blogs, websites and news reports are no less compelling for being modern. These people, too, are shaping the future, while fading to grey; becoming just another name on another page.

I hope that my husband's photographs will not fade so quickly. Andrew shares my fascination with Cambridge; even after 20 years he can still revisit and return with new and exciting images which capture the spirit of the city. He knows there will always be beauty to discover in Cambridge: it truly is a city for all seasons.

Debi Pearce, May 2017

Left: Clare College
Overleaf: Wisteria at Christ's College